I0824244

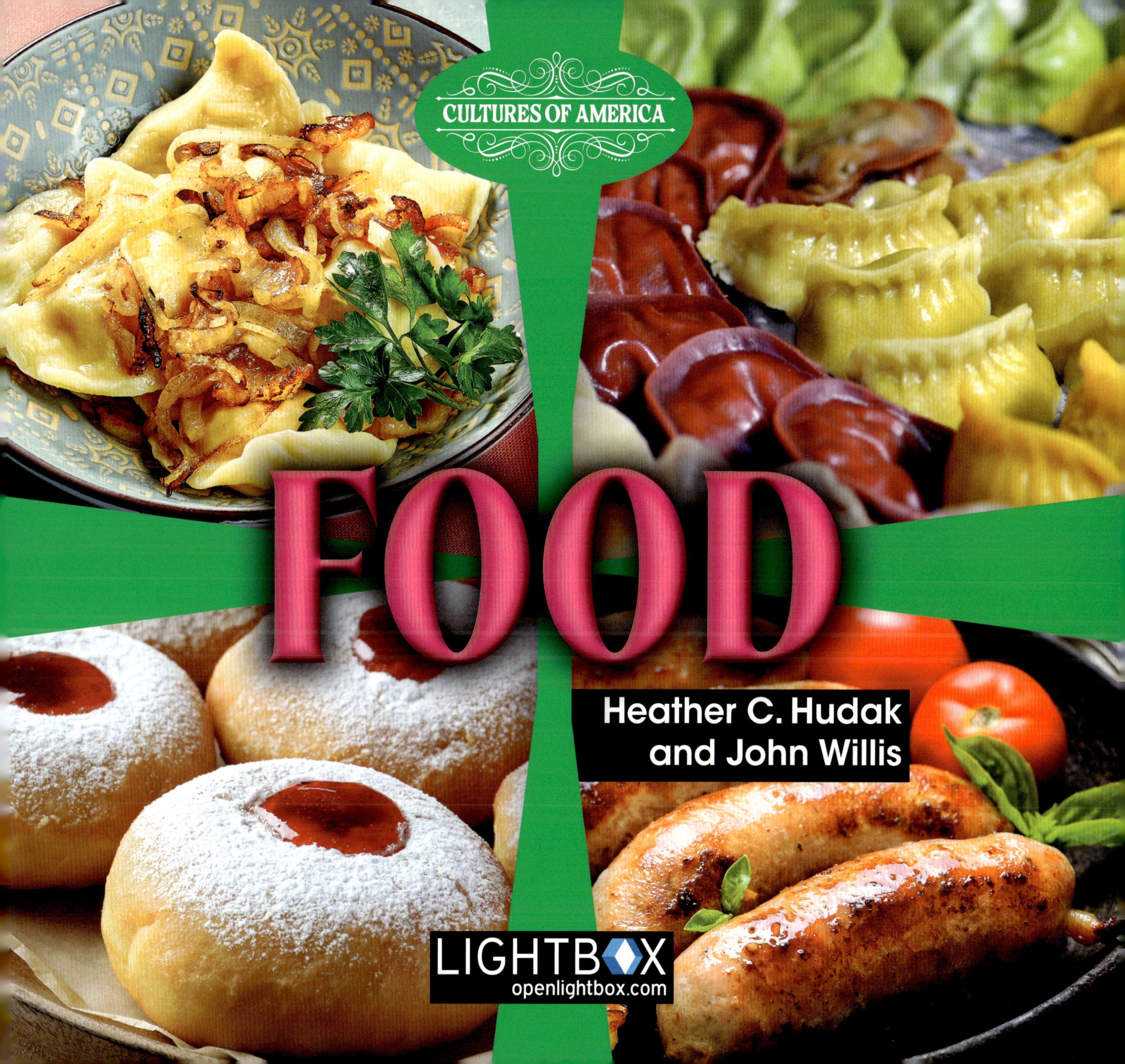
CULTURES OF AMERICA
FOOD
Heather C. Hudak
and John Willis
LIGHTBOX
openlightbox.com

LIGHTBOX

Go to **www.openlightbox.com** and enter this book's unique code.

ACCESS CODE

LBXU8644

Lightbox is an all-inclusive digital solution for the teaching and learning of curriculum topics in an original, groundbreaking way. Lightbox is based on National Curriculum Standards.

OPTIMIZED FOR

- ✓ TABLETS
- ✓ WHITEBOARDS
- ✓ COMPUTERS
- ✓ AND MUCH MORE!

STANDARD FEATURES OF LIGHTBOX

- **AUDIO** High-quality narration using text-to-speech system
- **VIDEOS** Embedded high-definition video clips
- **ACTIVITIES** Printable PDFs that can be emailed and graded
- **WEBLINKS** Curated links to external, child-safe resources
- **SLIDESHOWS** Pictorial overviews of key concepts
- **INTERACTIVE MAPS** Interactive maps and aerial satellite imagery
- **QUIZZES** Ten multiple choice questions that are automatically graded and emailed for teacher assessment
- **KEY WORDS** Matching key concepts to their definitions

SUPPLEMENTARY RESOURCES

- **SHARE** Share titles within your Learning Management System (LMS) or Library Circulation System
- **CURRICULUM** Find national and state curriculum correlations
- **CITATION** Create bibliographical references following the Chicago Manual of Style

VIDEOS

WEBLINKS

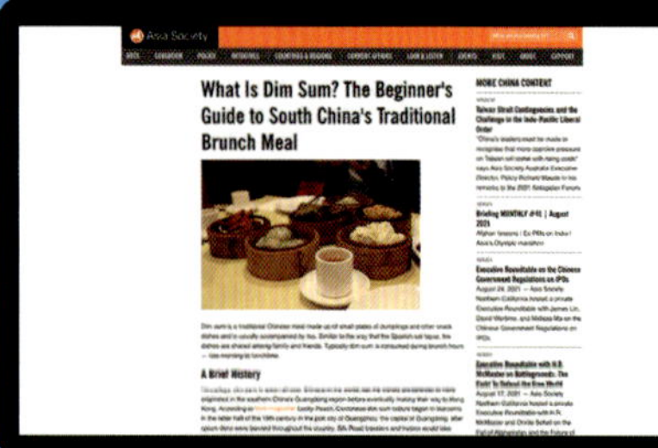

SLIDESHOWS

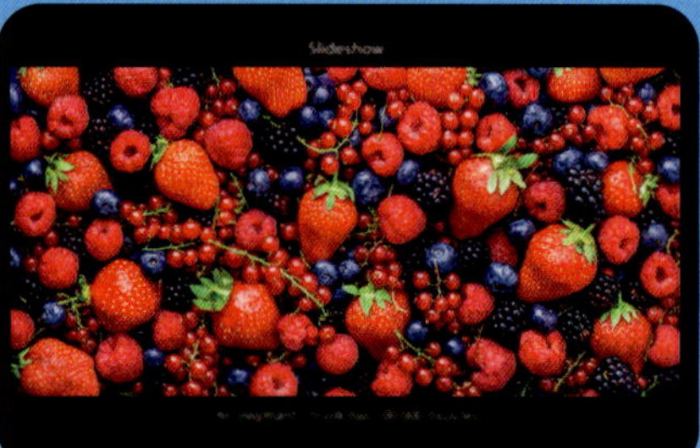

QUIZZES

This title is part of our Lightbox digital subscription

Lightbox Grades K–5 Subscription
ISBN 978-1-5105-5712-3

Access hundreds of Lightbox titles with our digital subscription. Sign up for a **FREE** subscription trial at **www.openlightbox.com/trial**

FOOD

CONTENTS

Ukrainian Dumplings

Perogies are dumplings in the shape of a half circle. They are made from dough that is filled with potato, cheese, meat, cabbage, or onions. Perogies can also be filled with fruit, such as blueberries. Most people eat several perogies at one meal. The dumplings are boiled or fried and served with butter, sour cream, bacon bits, mushrooms, or fried onions. The Ukrainian word for perogie is varenyky.

Borsch
Nalysnyky
Borsch is a type of beet soup.
What other foods can be made using beets?
Kovbasa
Holubtsi

Chinese Dim Sum

Yum cha, or dim sum, is a special way to serve a meal. It means "touch the heart." Dim sum meals include bite-sized buns that have a filling inside, noodles, steamed or fried dumplings, sweet pastries, vegetables, and meat. At dim sum, people are served about three to four of each food item. Each type of food is on its own plate. This lets people enjoy many types of food at one meal.

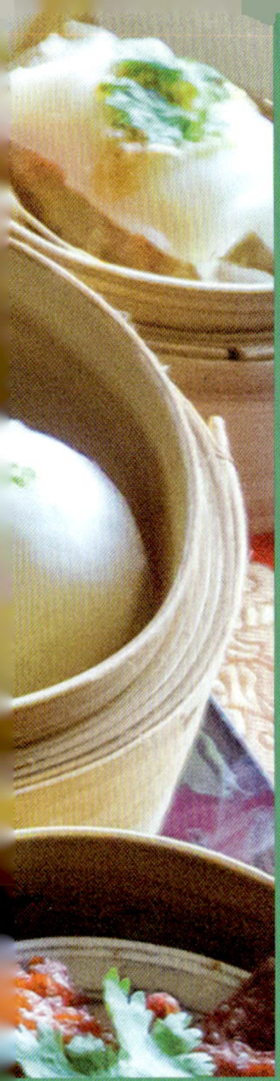

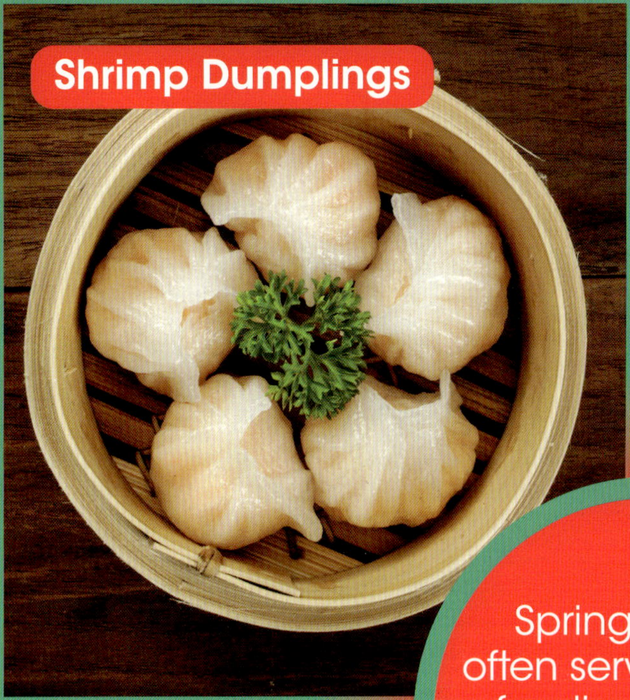
Shrimp Dumplings

Jasmine Tea

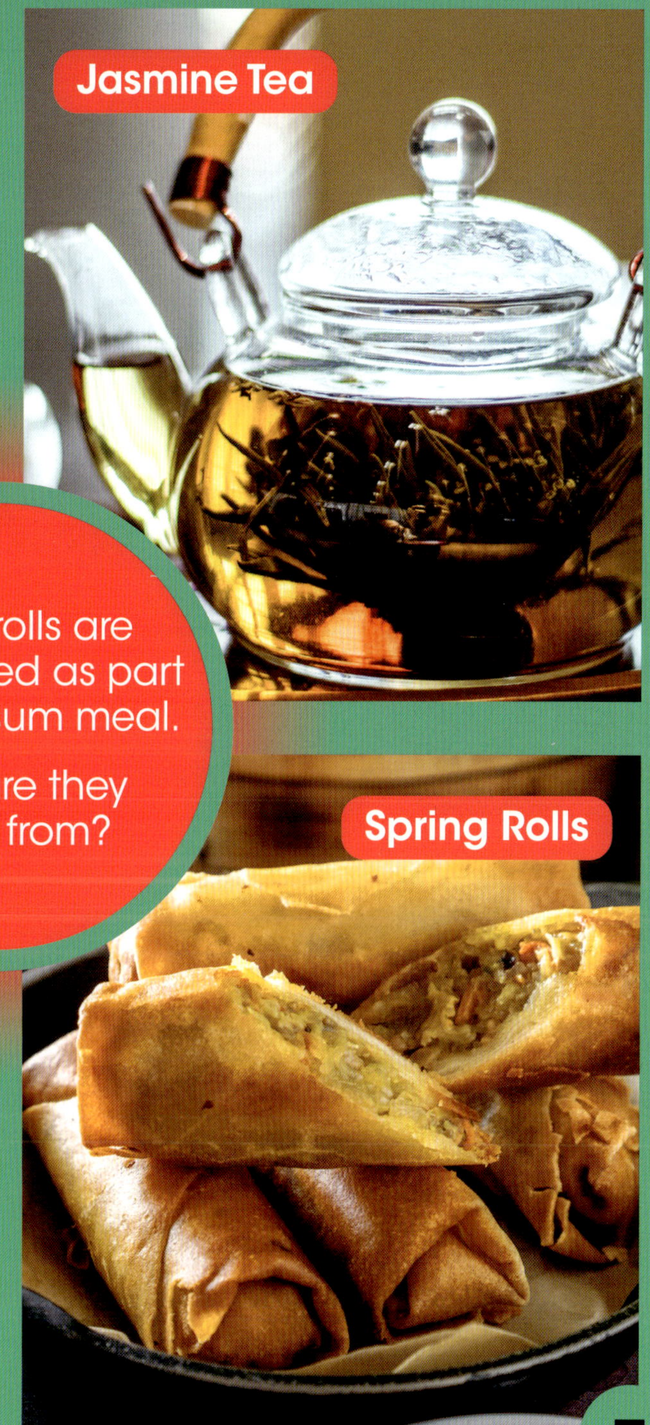

Spring rolls are often served as part of a dim sum meal.

What are they made from?

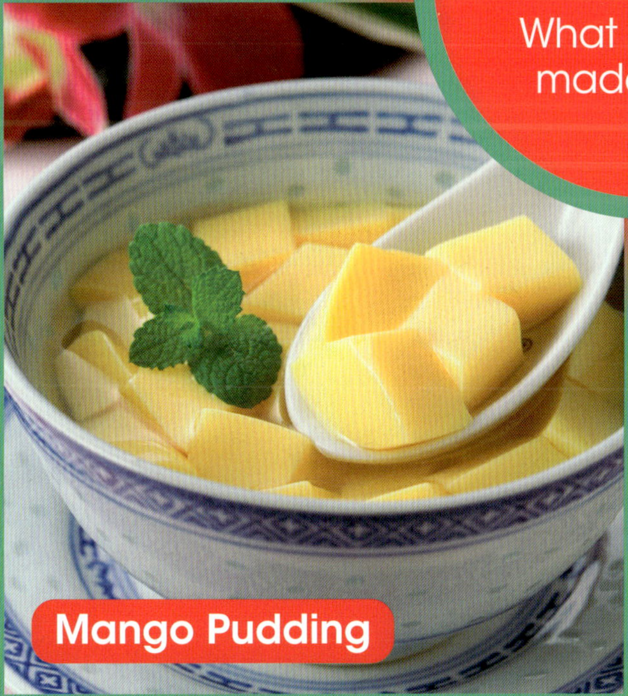
Mango Pudding

Spring Rolls

Native American Pemmican

Traditionally, pemmican was part of many Native American diets. It is made from a mixture of dried meat, animal fat, and berries or nuts. The mixture is mashed together and dried or stored in containers. It does not spoil, so it lasts a long time.

Traditionally, Native Americans hunted or gathered their food from nature.

What recipes do you know that use food from nature?

Jewish Baking

Bagels and stuffed pastries are common Jewish foods. Jewish people have been eating bagels for more than 400 years. A bagel is a type of bread that is shaped like a doughnut or ring. They are made from dough that is boiled in water and then baked. Sufganiyot are like jelly-filled doughnuts. They are made from a ball of dough that is fried and then filled with jelly or custard.

Matzah is part of many Jewish foods.

How is matzah made?

Creole Gumbo

Creole food is known for its seasoned flavors. It was developed in Louisiana. Creole food came from the mixing of many cultures. These include French, Spanish, and West African. One well-known Creole dish is gumbo. This is a type of stew. A Creole gumbo often has tomatoes, shellfish, and okra.

Creole gumbo often includes ingredients found in Louisiana.

What other ingredients are often used in stews?

German Sausage

Many people think of sauerkraut and wurst when they think of German food. Sauerkraut is made from chopped cabbage. The cabbage is then pickled. It has a sour flavor. Wurst is a type of sausage. It is made from ground meat and spices.

Many German foods are made using fruit.

Which foods pictured here have fruit inside?

Mexican Enchiladas

Today's Mexican food includes Central American ingredients, such as beans and corn. These are mixed with ingredients, such as rice and pork, that were first brought to Mexico from Spain. Enchiladas are Mexican foods made with meat, beans, or other ingredients. These are wrapped in thin, flat breads called tortillas. Enchiladas are served covered in sauce.

Food in Central America changed after the Spanish arrived.

How might your favorite foods have changed over time?

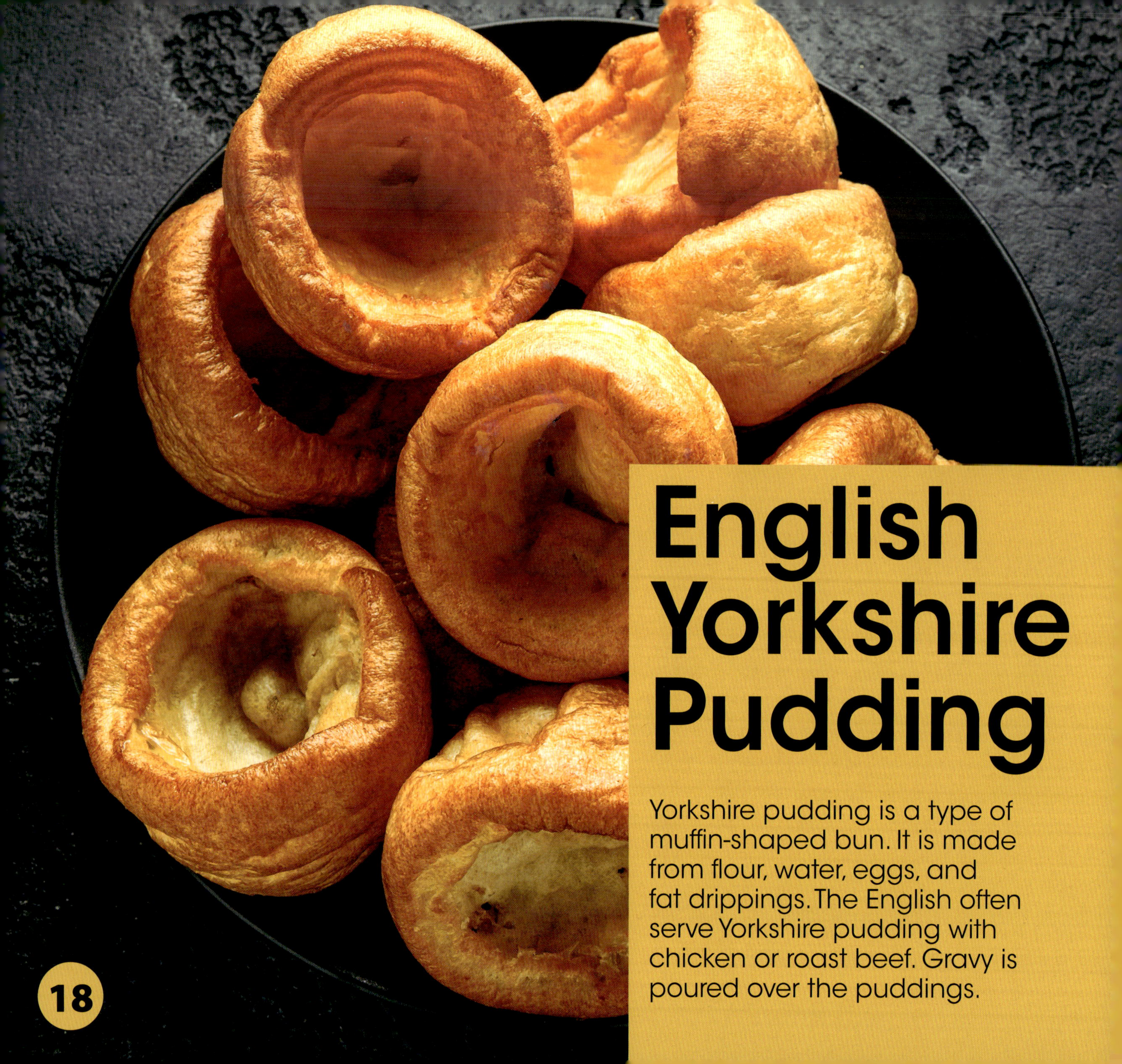

English Yorkshire Pudding

Yorkshire pudding is a type of muffin-shaped bun. It is made from flour, water, eggs, and fat drippings. The English often serve Yorkshire pudding with chicken or roast beef. Gravy is poured over the puddings.

Shepherd's pie is made from meat and vegetables covered with a layer of mashed potatoes.

Which other foods have layers?

Filipino Puto

Rice is an important food in the Philippines. It is eaten with most meals. One way Filipinos eat rice is called puto. Puto is a steamed rice cake. Rice is mixed with other ingredients to give puto a sweet flavor. Puto is spongy like angel cake. It is most often eaten as a dessert or for breakfast.

Rice is served at most Filipino meals.

Is there a food that you eat at most of your meals?

Matching Activity

You have learned about many kinds of food in the United States.

Match the name of each food below to the correct picture.

Creole Gumbo

English Yorkshire Pudding

Native American Pemmican

Chinese Dim Sum

Filipino Puto

Ukrainian Dumplings

Mexican Enchiladas

Jewish Baking

German Sausage

KEY WORDS

Research has shown that as much as 65 percent of all written material published in English is made up of 300 words. These 300 words cannot be taught using pictures or learned by sounding them out. They must be recognized by sight. This book contains 85 common sight words to help young readers improve their reading fluency and comprehension. This book also teaches young readers several important content words, such as proper nouns. These words are paired with pictures to aid in learning and improve understanding.

Page	Sight Words First Appearance
4	a, also, and, are, as, at, be, can, eat, for, from, in, is, made, most, of, one, or, people, such, that, the, they, with, word
5	foods, other, what
6	about, each, four, have, it, lets, many, means, on, this, three, to, way
7	often, part
8	American, animal, does, lasts, long, not, so, time, together, was
9	do, know, their, use, you
10	been, like, more, than, then, water, years
11	how
12	came, has, its, these
13	found
14	think, when
15	here, which
16	first, were
17	after, might, over, your
20	an, give, important
21	there

Page	Content Words First Appearance
4	bacon bits, blueberries, butter, cabbage, cheese, dough, dumplings, fruit, meal, meat, mushrooms, onions, perogies, potato, sour cream, varenyky
5	beets, borsch, holubtsi, kovbasa, nalysnyky, soup
6	buns, dim sum, heart, noodles, pastries, plate, yum cha
7	pudding, spring rolls, tea
8	berries, containers, diets, fat, nuts, pemmican
9	bannock, Native Americans, nature, recipes, rice, venison
10	bagels, custard, doughnut, jelly, ring, sufganiyot
11	blintz, challah, charoset, matzah ball
12	cultures, dish, gumbo, Louisiana, okra, shellfish, stew, tomatoes
13	bisque, étouffée, ingredients, jambalaya, pompano en papillote
14	sauerkraut, sausage, spices, wurst
15	schnitzel, spaetzle, stollen, strudel
16	beans, breads, corn, enchiladas, pork, sauce, Spain, tortillas
17	Central America, chiles en nogada, pico de gallo, tacos, tamales
18	chicken, eggs, gravy, roast beef, Yorkshire pudding
19	chips, crumpets, fish, shepherd's pie, trifle
20	angel cake, breakfast, dessert, Filipinos, Philippines, puto, rice cake
21	adobo, lumpia, sour shrimp stew, taho

Published by Lightbox Learning
276 5th Avenue, Suite 704 #917
New York, NY 10001
Website: www.openlightbox.com

Library of Congress Control Number available upon request.

ISBN 978-1-5105-6000-0 (hardcover)
ISBN 978-1-5105-6001-7 (multi-user eBook)

Printed in Guangzhou, China
1 2 3 4 5 6 7 8 9 0 25 24 23 22 21

092021
110820

Designer: Ana María Vidal Project Coordinator: John Willis

Every reasonable effort has been made to trace ownership and to obtain permission to reprint copyright material. The publisher would be pleased to have any errors or omissions brought to its attention so that they may be corrected in subsequent printings. The publisher acknowledges Alamy, Getty Images, and Shutterstock as the primary image suppliers for this title.